Contents

INTRODUCTION

AN OVERVIEW OF THE PARTY WALL ACT

THE PARTY WALL ACT 1996

Construction and repair of walls on line of junction

Section 1. New building on line of junction. 3

Section 2. Repair etc. of party wall: rights of owner. 8

Section 3. Party structure notices. 14

Section 4. Counter notices. 15

Section 5. Disputes arising under sections 3 and 4. 17

Adjacent excavation and construction

Section 6. Adjacent excavation and construction. 17

Rights etc.

Section 7. Compensation etc. 22

Section 8. Rights of entry. 24

Section 9. Easements. 25

Resolution of disputes

Section 10. Resolution of disputes. 26

Expenses

Section 11. Expenses. 32

Section 12. Security for expenses. 36

Section 13. Account for work carried out. 37

Section 14. Settlement of account 38

Miscellaneous

Section 15. Service of notices etc. 39

Section 16. Offences. 39

Section 17. Recovery of sums. 40

Section 18.	Exception in case of Temples etc.	40
Section 19.	The Crown.	41
Section 20.	Interpretation.	42
Section 21.	Other statutory provisions.	46

General

Section 22.	Short title, commencement and extent.	46

A Guide to the Act

Points to be considered when you are a building owner or adjoining owner's surveyor 48

Appendices	Notices	51
	Letters of appointment	61
	An Award	65
	A schedule of condition	69

Index 75

INTRODUCTION

The aim of this book is to explain how the requirements of the Act affect owners and occupiers of property when they come to deal with party walls, boundary walls of all types and deep excavations close to adjoining properties and boundaries. The reader will be given a surveyor's interpretation of the Act by annotations of its provisions drawn from his experience, reading and anecdotal information gained from a lifetime of "hands on".

The Party Wall etc Act 1996 effectively re-enacts the London Building Acts (Amendment) Act 1939, but the new Act contains new obligations and has amended the original Act in several different, and subtle ways. Section 1(5) of the Act introduces for the first time an obligation for an owner to inform his neighbours if he intends digging an excavation near other owners land. The Act sets out a clear framework for the administration of all the various rights and duties. While they take time to implement the time periods are reasonable and the Act builds upon two hundred years of experience of dealing with contentious issues in Central London.

In the paragraphs below I refer to owners surveyors by the reference to "he". This also includes reference to "she", "them", "it" or "he". The Act uses the masculine gender in its text and I have followed this for clarity.

Before you start reading the Act, please take the time to read the definitions in section 20 of the Act. You will find some of the terminology strange, so please get used to the terms building owner and adjoining owner.

An overview of the Party Wall etc Act 1996

The 1996 Party Wall etc Act which applies to the whole of England and Wales effectively re-enacts (with minor variations and amendments) the London Building (Amendment) Act 1939 Part IV which in its turn re-enacted the London Building Act of 1930 and1894. The Party Wall etc. Act came into effect on 1 July 1997.

The history of party walls in central London goes back at least 800 years and the legislation arose because of the need to try and prevent the spread of fire. Over the years the legislation was aimed at providing a fire break between buildings but it seems that it was largely ignored or unenforceable until the disastrous Great Fire of London in 1666. In 1667 the Prevention of Fire Metropolis Act gave teeth to the authorities and from then on walls between properties were generally built of non-combustible material.

Readers should remember that most medieval buildings were timber framed, often thatched and were generally only separated by thin timber framed walls infilled with straw, wattle or daub. A wonderful opportunity for fire to spread laterally with little hindrance!

In the nineteenth century, a series of Acts were passed which refined owners rights and enlarged the ability of owners to control what, where and how works were carried to walls in shared ownership, or walls which were built as boundary walls or were proposed to be built as either.

The 1939 Act clarified all the various pieces of legislation and in London it has been a pragmatic method of proactively dealing with boundary matters of all sorts. Its common sense approach to foreseeable problems has allowed surveyors to resolve ongoing construction difficulties and has allowed the Central London area to be developed without undue difficulties.

I think it is significant that the implementation of the various Acts has for approximately 200 years rested in the hands of appointed surveyors. No definition of the term "surveyor" has ever been attempted in any of the Acts, but effectively each party to a boundary dispute appoints his/her surveyor who then has the power under the "Acts" to resolve the matter. If the respective owner who has appointed him does not like the concluded Award/agreement he/she has the right of appeal to the Courts. This has focused owners attentions on the detail and has largely eliminated petty procrastination.

The Act has worked in the London area because of reasonable exercise of the rights given by it. These rights go beyond common law and equity and have to be exercised carefully. A skilled surveyor will ensure he meets the parties he is dealing with and explains in simple terms what is proposed. By the use of personality, experience and professionalism surveyors have resolved most boundary matters and relatively few cases have ended up in the Courts following the introduction of the 1939 Act.

The new Act is a code for being a good neighbour and by its use unnecessary disputes, aggravation and unhappiness will be avoided. It is a sound pragmatic tool for getting work carried out and protecting the rights of those who are subject the works.

Party Wall Act

An Act to make the provision in respect of party walls, and excavation and construction in proximity to certain buildings or structures; and for connected purposes.

[18th July 1996]

Be it enacted by the Queen's most Excellent Majesty, by and with the advice and consent of the Lords Spiritual and Temporal, and Commons, in this present Parliament assembled, and by the authority of the same, as follows:–

The word "etc" refers to matters which do not deal with party walls specifically. The Act also includes provisions to deal with boundary walls, excavation abutting buildings and excavations close to buildings.

English language scholars may not appreciate the use of the word "etc" in the title but a fully inclusive title for the Act would probably be confusing.

Construction and repair of walls on line of junction

1.–(1) This section shall have effect where lands of different owners adjoin and–

(a) are not built on at the line of the junction; or

(b) are built on at the line of junction only to the extent of a boundary wall (not being a party fence wall or the external wall of a building),

and either owner is about to build on any part of the line of junction.

Section 1

This section incorporates into the Act proposals to build walls on or over the boundary line; it applies where no walls exist or where there is a wall built wholly on one owners land.

Practice Notes

(1) In the Act there is no definition of the words "line of junction".

My interpretation is that the "line of junction" is the boundary between the properties. The "line of junction" may or may not have a physical presence (fence, wall, ditch, etc) but by reference to title deeds it is often possible to identify where it should be. However, title deeds and any plans attached to them are not necessarily accurate so it is essential to carefully research the situation if there is any doubt.

These words are carefully chosen given the writers experience of boundary disputes.

(2) Please see sections 1(2) and 1(3) for serving notices and kicking off the procedures.

(2) If a building owner desires to build a party wall or party fence wall on the line of junction he shall, at least one month before he intends the building work to start, serve on any adjoining owner a notice which indicates his desire to build and describes the intended wall.

Section 1(2)

Before an owner can exercise his rights he has to serve the notice.

This section applies to situations where the owner wishes to build over the line of junction.

Practice Note

It is important to understand the difference between building up to a boundary and over it.

Over it - use s1(2)

Upto it - use s1(5)

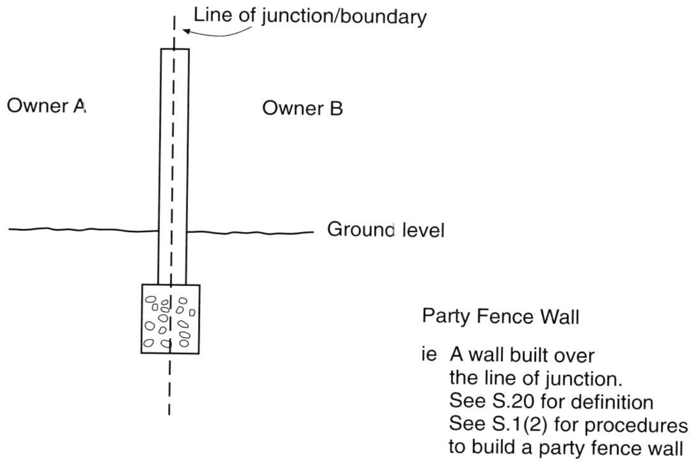

(3) If, having been served with notice described in subsection (2), an adjoining owner serves on the building owner a notice indicating his consent to the building of a party wall or party fence wall–

(a) the wall shall be built half on the land of each of the two owners or in such other position as may be agreed between the two owners; and

(b) the expense of building the wall shall be from time to time defrayed by the two owners in such proportion as has regard to the use made or to be made of the wall by each of them and to the cost of labour and materials prevailing at the time when that use is made by each owner respectively.

Section 1(3)
The recipient of the notice (adjoining owner) may agree to the proposed works. If so, the detail of the construction will need to be agreed.

In addition, the cost sharing arrangements will have to be resolved.

<u>Practice Note</u>
If the wall is more than 2 metres high, part of a listed building or in a conservation area be aware of statutory constraints under the Planning Acts of building such walls.

The detail of the wall will reflect the two owners wishes. However both parties may want something different and the cost sharing arrangements will reflect this. Costs/payments will reflect use of the wall and the respective owners detailed requirements.

(4) If, having been served with notice described in subsection (2), an adjoining owner does not consent under this subsection to the building of a party wall or party fence wall, the building owner may only build the wall–

(a) at his own expense; and
(b) as an external wall or a fence wall, as the case may be, placed wholly on his own land,

and consent under this subsection is consent by a notice served within the period of fourteen days beginning with the day on which the notice described in subsection (2) is served.

Section 1(4)
A building owner cannot build the wall over the junction line unless the adjoining owner agrees within 14 days.

If there is no consent the building owner can only build on his own land and to do this he must serve notice under section 1(5).

<u>Practice Note</u>
(1) As a surveyor encourage owners to discuss the matter directly and try to "agree" before serving the notice.

2) If there is any doubt, building owners should serve notices under subsections 1(2) and 1(5) using two different notices. This will allow the construction of the "boundary wall", if the owner next door does not want a "party fence wall".

(5) If the building owner desires to build on the line of junction a wall placed wholly on his own land he shall, at least one month before he intends the building work to start, serve on any adjoining owner a notice which indicates his desire to build and describes the intended wall.

Section 1(5)

This provision is new to party wall/boundary wall legislation and is intended to put adjoining owners on notice that a wall is to be built. Excavation for the wall could affect the stability of an owner's land, adjoining shed, gardens, plants, trees etc.

Practice Note

By following the Act procedures owners serving the notice under section 1(5) have a right of access to do the work. This prevents building the walls over hand.

When exercising the right of access it is essential and good practice to: (1) erect a hoarding around the new wall to limit intrusion; (2) carefully record the boundary line/line of junction/legal boundary to ensure the new wall is constructed precisely in the right position; (3) ensure the adjoining owner is left as you find him.

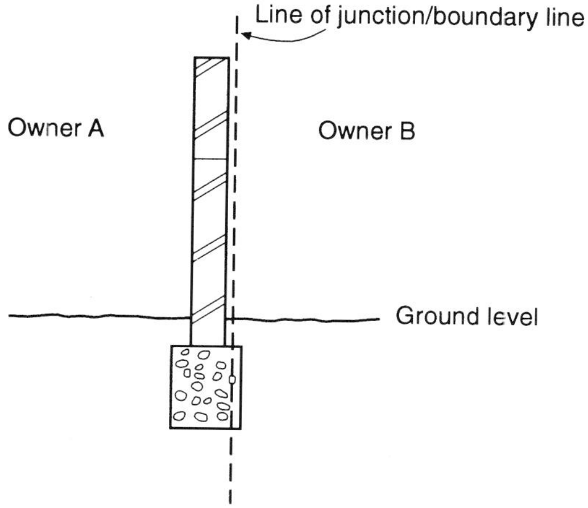

A boundary wall : See section 1.5 for procedures to build a new boundary wall (not a party fence wall)

(6) Where the building owner builds a wall wholly on his own land in accordance with subsection (4) or (5) he shall have the right, at any time in the period which–

(a) begins one month after the day on which the notice mentioned in the subsection concerned was served, and

(b) ends twelve months after that day,

to place below the level of the land of the adjoining owner such projecting footings and foundations as are necessary for the construction of the wall.

Section 1(6)

This section allows a building owner constructing a wall wholly on his land to put foundations necessary for the wall under the land of the adjoining owner.

This legalises what otherwise would be a trespass.

The word "necessary" is difficult to interpret but if the wall has traditional strip concrete foundations the writer's view is that this is necessary and permitted by the Act.

Practice Note
Ensure full details of the wall and its foundations are clearly shown on the appropriate drawings.

(7) Where the building owner builds a wall wholly on his own land in accordance with subsection (4) or (5) he shall do so at his own expense and shall compensate any adjoining owner and any adjoining occupier for any damage to his property occasioned by–

(a) the building of the wall;
(b) the placing of any footings or foundations placed in accordance with subsection (5).

Section 1(7)
The building owner has to ensure as far as he can that in exercising his rights he causes no damage but if he does he has to pay for remedying the damage. Trees, paths, gardens, sheds, external lighting and irrigation systems may be affected by the works. Often it is prudent for the building owner to pay the adjoining owner to have these items moved, altered, reinstated by the adjoining owners own contractors.

Practice Note
Survey the area affected and find out at first hand what works will be necessary to prevent damage and what enabling works are required.

(8) Where any dispute arises under this section between the building owner and any adjoining owner or occupier it is to be determined in accordance with section 10.

Section 1(8)
It is possible for owners to agree on every item in respect of a s.1 matter and an owner having served Notice begins the work which proceeds smoothly to completion with no disagreement.

However if an adjoining owner is concerned with any matter he can be represented and the surveyors appointed should deal with disputed item/items by entering into an Award (a written agreement for the works to proceed). See section 10 for dealing with disputes.

Practice Note
In the writer's experience a majority of works initiated by Notice end up with surveyors being appointed and an Award being agreed/signed and delivered to the respective owners.

Repair etc. of party wall: rights of owner

2.–(1) This section applies where lands of different owners adjoin and at the line of junction the said lands are built on or a boundary wall, being a party fence wall or the external wall of a building, has been erected.

> **Section 2(1)**
>
> *This section gives owners extensive rights to carry out works where the boundary line is built on.*
>
> *The form of construction can be any one of the following:*
>
> *(a a boundary wall built over the boundary – known as a party fence wall;*
>
> *(b) a building where the external wall is built on the line of junction;*
>
> *(c) a party wall which separates buildings in different ownerships.*
>
> *Please refer to s.20 for definitions of party walls and party fence walls.*
>
> *Practice Note*
>
> *These rights are the most likely ones to be subject to the procedures under the Act and they have to be exercised carefully. The various rights/obligations are set out in s.2 subsections below and apply to buildings, boundary walls, party walls, party structures.*

(2) A building owner shall have the following rights–

(a) to underpin, thicken or raise a party structure, a party fence wall, or an external wall which belongs to the building owner and is built against a party structure or party fence wall.

> **Section 2(2)(a)**
>
> *Paragraph (a) allows all these types of "party wall" (see 2(1) above) to be*
>
> *(1) raised*
>
> *(2) thickened*
>
> *(3) underpinned.*
>
> *Practice Note*
>
> *Approval under the Act for these works will be only one of several issues a building owner has to consider. The works will be subject to consideration under other statutory provisions to include:*
>
> *(1) Town and Country Planning Acts – planning permission*
>
> *(2) Listed buildings consent;*
>
> *(3) Building Regulations approval.*
>
> *Underpinning usually involves taking the walls and their foundations deeper into the ground.*
>
> *Underpinning will normally involve the whole thickness of the wall and this is permitted/authorised by the Act.*

(b) to make good, repair, or demolish and rebuild, a party structure or party fence wall in a case where such work is necessary on account of defect or want of repair of the structure or wall.

Section 2(2)(b)
Either owner has the right to take down and rebuild a party wall or part of it due to disrepair.

If the wall is not fit for either owner the owners would normally share the cost of reconstruction in proportion to the use they made of the party wall/party fence wall

(c) to demolish a partition which separates buildings belonging to different owners but does not conform with statutory requirements and to build instead a party wall which does so conform;

(d) in the case of buildings connected by arches or structures over public ways or over passages belonging to other persons, to demolish the whole or part of such buildings, arches or structures which do not conform with statutory requirements and to rebuild them so that they do so conform;

Section 2(2)(c) & (d)
The right to rebuild partitions as party walls and arches/structures over public ways/passages is an incorporation of old clauses from previous legislation.

In over 30 years experience the writer has not seen these clauses implemented but he suspects they have their origin in Victorian times. Section 2(8) below should be referred to because structures which conformed to the regulations when the Act was passed are deemed to conform to the regulations on the date they were erected.

(e) to demolish a party structure which is of insufficient strength or height for the purposes of any intended building of the building owner and to rebuild it of sufficient strength or height for the said purposes (including rebuilding to a lesser height or thickness where the rebuilt structure is of sufficient strength and height for the purposes of any adjoining owner);

Section 2(2)(e)
This right is subject to onerous obligations in clause 2(4)(a) and (b) below.

<u>Practice Note</u>
The right to demolish and rebuild a party structure which is of insufficient strength or height is a considerable undertaking. Any owner proposing to do this will incur extraordinary costs and it should be considered only as a last option.

An owner should consider all the other options open to him, namely underpinning, repair or a strengthening scheme under sections 2(2)(a) and (b) above.

(f) to cut into a party structure for any purpose (which may be or include the purpose of inserting a damp proof course;

Section 2(2)(f)

This useful clause allows a building owner to cut into a wall for numerous purposes.

Normally it is used for putting padstones and beams into party walls.

The clause specifically includes a damp proof course and this can take the form of a thin sheet of impervious material or injected chemicals.

While the clause refers to any purpose the "cutting in" must be in compliance with normal statutory constraints.

The building owner has to make good any damage etc. See clause 2(5) below.

(g) to cut away from a party wall, party fence wall, external wall or boundary wall any footing or any projecting chimney breast, jamb or flue, or other projection on or over the land of the building owner in order to erect, raise or underpin any such wall or for any other purpose;

Section 2(2)(g)

This right to cut away projections, allows a building owner to build any of the following

(a) a wall on the boundary

(b) a party wall

(c) a party fence wall

(d) an external wall.

Practice Note

However the right can only be exercised in accordance with sound building practice and not in any way to the detriment of the adjoining owner.

The building owner has to make good any damage etc. See subsection 2(5) below.

(h) to cut away or demolish parts of any wall or building of an adjoining owner overhanging the land of the building owner or overhanging a party wall, to the extent that it is necessary to cut away or demolish the parts to enable a vertical wall to be erected or raised against the wall or building of the adjoining owner.

Section 2(2)(h)

This right extends to cutting away any projection in order to build/raise a party wall or external wall.

If the offending projection is the eaves of a roof or a box gutter sitting over a party wall the building owner has the right to cut them off and raise the wall/ a new wall. However any owner exercising this right has to make good.

(j) to cut into the wall of an adjoining owner's building in order to insert a flashing or other weather-proofing of a wall erected against that wall;

Section 2(2)(j)

This allows an owner to cut a flashing into an adjoining owners wall and this will eliminate open voids between abutting buildings.

This is a most welcome addition to boundary wall/party wall legislation.

(k) to execute any other necessary works incidental to the connection of a party structure with the premises adjoining it;

Section 2(2)(k)

This allows an owner to connect the party wall to the adjoining premises.

The uses of this section are numerous but the provision of lateral restraint to an exposed party wall can be a most useful way of stablising a party structure.

(l) to raise a party fence wall, or to raise such a wall for use as a party wall, and to demolish a party fence wall and rebuild it as a party fence wall or as a party wall;

Section 2(2)(l)

This allows building owners, subject to other statutory consents to use a party fence wall as a party wall or rebuild it as a party wall.

This right will allow an owner to take down a party fence wall and rebuild it as part of an extension to the house, building etc.

(m) subject to the provisions of section 11(7), to reduce, or to demolish and rebuild, a party wall or party fence wall to–

(i) a height of not less than two metres where the wall is not used by an adjoining owner to any greater extent than a boundary wall; or

(ii) a height currently enclosed upon by the building of an adjoining owner;

Section 2(2)(m)

An owner under these provisions may demolish rebuild or reduce a party wall/party fence wall to a height of 2 metres or the height currently used to ensure the adjoining owners building is maintained in its present condition.

An owner therefore cannot remove a party fence wall/party wall without agreement but can reduce it in height.

Where adjoining old buildings have been demolished "tall" party walls can be left. This "new" clause allows such a wall to be reduced in height subject to agreement.

(n) to expose a party wall or party structure hitherto enclosed subject to providing adequate weathering.

Section 2(2)(n)
This allows an owner to demolish his building exposing the party wall to the weather. The debate on what constitutes adequate weathering will depend on the time of the wall is to be exposed and where it is. The writer can envisage no requirement to weather the wall or the need to provide felt battens and tile hanging in a seaside location fronting the prevailing weather.

(3) Where work mentioned in paragraph (a) of subsection (2) is not necessary on account of defect or want of repair of the structure or wall concerned, the right falling within that paragraph is exercisable:–

(a) subject to making good all damage occasioned by the work to the adjoining premises or to their internal furnishings and decorations; and
(b) where the work is to a party structure or external wall, subject to carrying out relevant flues and chimney stacks up to such a height and in such materials as may be agreed between the building owner and the adjoining owner concerned or, in the event of dispute, determined in accordance with section 10;

and relevant flues and chimney stacks are those which belong to an adjoining owner and either form part of or rest on or against the party structure or external wall.

Section 2(3)
These sections relate to work carried out under paragraph (a) of subsection 2 when disrepair is not involved. The building owner is carrying out the work for his own purposes and he is liable for any making good and any damage to the adjoining owners premises.

(4) The right falling within subsection 2(e) is exercisable subject to:–

(a) making good all damage occasioned by the work to the adjoining premises or to their internal furnishings and decorations; and
(b) Carrying any relevant flues and chimney stacks up to such a height and in such materials as may be agreed between the building owner and the adjoining owner concerned or, in the event of dispute, determined in accordance with section 10;

and relevant flues and chimney stacks are those which belong to and adjoining owner and either form part of or rest on or against the party structure.

Section 2(4)
The conditions of exercising clause 2(e) are clearly set out in this clause. The cost of raising flues can be considerable and the writer has seen them raised in an asbestos based material above a listed building in Poland Street W1. The raising of these flues dated from the 1930's and the work was carried out prior to the Listed Building Legislation.

(5) Any right falling within subsection (2)(f), (g) or (h) is exercisable subject to making good all damage occasioned by the work to the adjoining premises or to their internal furnishings and decorations.

Section 2(5)
This Act and its predecessors make an owner responsible for putting right any damage his works cause. Effectively, he must leave this neighbour as he finds him, even if the damage is inevitable he is under a strict obligation to reinstate or pay for the reinstatement.

To protect the interests of both parties the surveyors/owners should record in writing and by photograph the existing condition of the buildings, which are likely to be affected by the works. This "schedule of condition" is then attached to the agreement/Award agreed by the parties. Even if there is no agreement/Award it is essential in my view to record the condition of the adjoining owners building before work starts.

The form of a schedule of condition can vary to suit the circumstances but in the appendices I have set out a typical example.

(6) The right falling within subsection (2)(j) is exercisable subject to making good all damage occasioned by the work to the wall of the adjoining owner's building.

Section 2(6)
Please see clause s.2(5) above.

An owner is responsible for making good any damage and the "schedule of condition" will set the benchmark for resolving the matter.

(7) The right falling within subsection (2)(m) is exercisable subject to:–

(a) reconstructing any parapet or replacing an existing parapet with another one; or
(b) construction a parapet where one is needed but did not exist before.

Section 2(7)
If a wall is reduced in height or rebuilt to a lower level and a parapet is required then the building owner must provide one. It may require the provision of copings or the salvage and reuse of copings in case of Listed Buildings.

(8) For the purposes of this section a building or structure which was erected before the day on which this Act was passed shall be deemed to conform with statutory requirements if it conforms with the statutes regulating buildings or structures on the date which it was erected.

Section 2(8)
For the purposes of subsection 2 of the Act the structure is deemed to have been constructed in accordance with statutory requirements if it complied with them when it was originally built. As building regulations can change several times in the life time of a building this clause removes the need to rebuild a structure or part if it no longer complies.

Party structure notices

3.–(1) Before exercising any right conferred on him by section 2 a building owner shall serve on any adjoining owner a notice (in this Act referred to as a "party structure notice") stating:–

(a) the name and address of the building owner;
(b) the nature and particulars of the proposed work including, in cases where the building owner proposed to construct special foundations, plans, sections and details of construction of the special foundations together with reasonable particulars of the loads to be carried thereby; and
(c) the date on which the proposed work will begin.

Section 3(1)
The Act gives owners their rights under s.2 but they cannot be used unless A NOTICE is served. No particular form of Notice is specifically required but to be valid it should give the details listed above and be clear to a lay person that it is a Notice under the Act.

Practice Note
In multi occupied buildings tracing all the various owners (freeholders and lessees) can be difficult but a visit to the neighbouring property with an explanation usually provides the information.

The Notice should include as much detail of the work as possible which is relevant to the 'structure'.

Special foundations can only be constructed where an adjoining owner gives his express consent. Therefore, all the details and structural calculations are normally provided if a positive response is to be achieved where consent for special foundations is sought.

(2) A party structure notice shall:–

(a) be served at least two months before the date on which the proposed work will begin;
(b) cease to have effect if the work to which it relates:–

(i) has not begun within the period of twelve months beginning with the day on which the notice is served; and
(ii) is not prosecuted with due diligence.

Section 3(2)
To be valid a Party Structure Notice under section 2 must be served at least two months before work is due to commence. Notices have a life of twelve months and they expire if they are served and there is no follow up within a reasonable period.

(3) Nothing in this section shall:–
(a) prevent a building owner from exercising with the consent in writing of the adjoining owners and of the adjoining occupiers any right conferred on him by section 2; or
(b) require a building owner to serve any party structure notice before complying with any notice served under any statutory provisions relating to dangerous or neglected structures.

Section 3(3)
(a) If an owner serves a Notices and the adjoining owner/s agree in writing, the works can proceed immediately.

This can be achieved in a surprisingly large number of cases where time is taken to meet neighbours, explain the work in detail and then serve the Notice.

(b) In the event of danger, the provisions of the Act as to 'Notices' does not apply. However, the dangerous situations has to be official with the receipt of a formal dangerous Structure Notice from a Local Authority.

Practice Note
If the owners agree the work can proceed as in s.3(3)(a) it is prudent to record the condition of the adjoining owners building and produce a 'schedule of condition'. This reduces the chances of a dispute if there is damage as a result of the work.

Counter notices

4.–(1) An adjoining owner may, having been served with a Party Structure Notice serve on the building owner a notice (in this Act referred to as a "counter notice") setting out:–
(a) In respect of a Party Fence Wall or Party Structure, a requirement that the building owner build in or on the wall or structure to which the notice relates such chimney copings, breasts, jambs or flues, or such piers or recesses or other like works, as may reasonably be required for the convenience of the adjoining owner;
(b) In respect of special foundations to which the adjoining owner consents under section 7(4) below, a requirement that the special foundations:–

(i) be placed at a special greater depth than that proposed by the building owner; or

(ii) be constructed of sufficient strength to bear the load to be carried by columns of any intended building of the adjoining owner,

or both.

> **Section 4(1)**
> *(a) The ability to serve a counter notice and ensure the adjoining owner can have features he wants is a sensible provision.*
>
> *It is also wholly compatible with the notion of a party wall as a "jointly owned" structure.*
>
> *The costs of the new party fence wall with the additional features asked for by the adjoining owner have to be calculated by reference to s11(9); the adjoining owner has to pay for the features he has requested.*

(2) A counter notice shall:–

(a) specify the works required by the notice to be executed and shall be accompanied by plans, sections and particulars of such works; and

(b) be served within the period of one month beginning with the day on which the Party Structure Notice is served.

> **Section 4(2)**
> *The terms and timing of the counter notice are clearly set out in this subsection. The one month time limit is designed to avoid undue delay. As an adjoining owner has to pay for the features he wants and detail them the writer is not aware of any example of counter notices having been served as a delaying tactic.*

(3) A building owner on whom a counter notice has been served shall comply with the requirements of the counter notice unless the execution of the works required by the counter notice would:–

(a) be injurious to him;

(b) cause unnecessary inconvenience to him; or

(c) cause unnecessary delay in the execution of the works pursuant to the Party Structure Notice.

> **Section 4(3)**
> *If a building owner wishes to avoid carrying out the works in a counter notice, he will have to prove his case under either (a) (b) or (c). Because the adjoining owner has to pay for his requirements the onus will be on the building owner to show he cannot reasonably do the work.*

Disputes arising under sections 3 and 4

5. If an owner on whom a party structure notice or a counter notice has been served does not serve a notice indicating his consent to it within the period of fourteen days beginning with the day on which the Party Structure Notice or counter notice was served, he shall be deemed to have dissented from the notice and dispute shall be deemed to have arisen between the parties.

Section 5
Failure to reply to a notice implies dissent and from experience the time scale of fourteen days has the following consequences.

(i) it focuses people's attention on the Notice.

(ii) it allows the building owner (after fourteen days) to set in motion the Act procedures for default – see s.10.

Adjoining owners quite often do not like to be associated with a dispute and agree to work proceeding under s.3(3)(a).

Adjacent excavation and construction

6.–(1) This section applies where:–

(a) a building owner proposed to excavate, or excavate for and erect a building or structure, within a distance of three metres measured horizontally from any part of a building or structure of an adjoining owner and;

(b) any part of the proposed excavation, building or structure will within those three metres extend to a lower level than the level of the bottom of the foundations of the building or structure of the adjoining owner.

Section 6(1)
The obligations placed on the building owner in this section are designed to prevent undermining of foundations and loss of lateral restraint to adjoining buildings.

Please refer to the diagrams provided for a clear explanation of this '3 metre rule'.

From experience, this requirement is a practical safeguard for those with construction knowledge. However, there have been cases when a layman excavates under his house to form a cellar does not support the excavation and his house and his neighbour's have suffered damage.

The rule is if your building works are within 3 metres and at a lower level than the adjoining owners building, the building owner must serve a notice. Ignorance is no excuse.

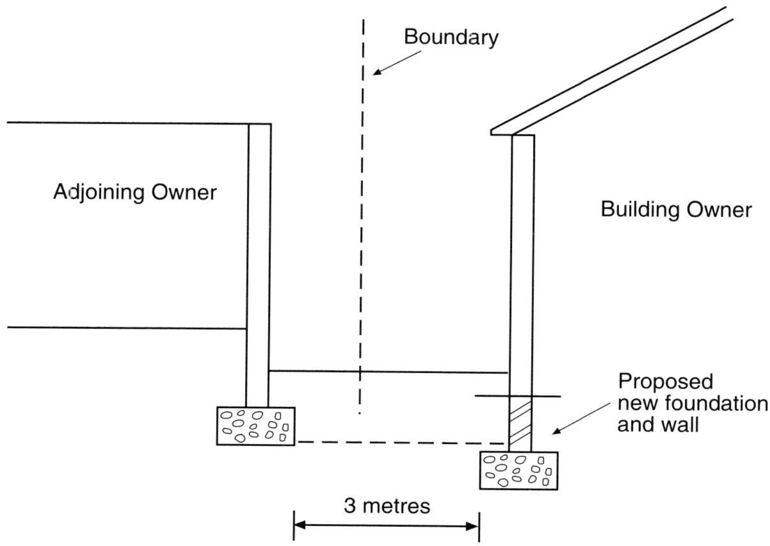

Within 3 metres and at a lower level, notice must be served

(2) This section also applies where:–

(a) a building owner proposes to excavate, or excavate for and erect a building or structure, within a distance of six metres measured horizontally from any part of a building or structure of an adjoining owner; and

(b) any part of the proposed excavation, building or structure will within those six metres meet a plane drawn downwards in the direction of the excavation, building or structure of the building owners at an angle of forty-five degrees to the horizontal from the line formed by the intersection of the plane of the level of the bottom of the foundations of the building or structure of the adjoining owner with the plane of the external face of the external wall of the building or structure of the adjoining owner.

Section 6.2

As with s.6(1)(a)&(b) this section is designed to protect adjoining owners. Please refer to the diagram to show how this section applies.

Because pile foundations can go deep into the ground, the implications are that there can be two or more buildings with owners/occupiers affected by the works.

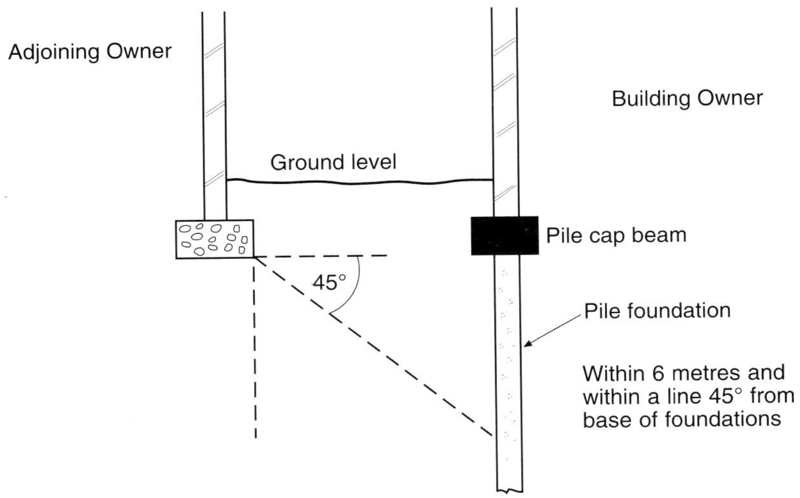

(3) The building owners may, and if required by the adjoining owner shall, at his own expense, underpin or otherwise strengthen or safeguard the foundations of the building or structure of the adjoining owners so far as may be necessary.

> **Section 6.3**
> *On receipt of a section 6 Notice, an adjoining owner will need to consider the matter carefully and in the writer's view, he should seek professional assistance. His adviser/surveyor/engineer will need to assess the situation and advise on any necessary safeguarding, underpinning or other works to protect the adjoining owners premises. The adjoining owner must then communicate this information in writing to the building owner.*
>
> *Any necessary work will be paid for by the building owner.*

(4) Where the buildings or structure of different owners are within the respective distances mentioned in subsections (1) and (2) the owners of those buildings or structures shall be deemed to be adjoining owners for the purposes of this section.

> **Section 6(4)**
> *The distances, not ownership of the land, govern who should be served with a notice. Therefore, a narrow passageway between the building owner and an adjoining building will not remove the building owners obligation to serve a notice on his neighbours who are either within 3 metres or 6 metres.*

(5) In any case where this section applies the building owner shall, at least one month before beginning to excavate, or excavate for an erect a building or structure, serve on the adjoining owner a notice indicating his proposals and stating whether he proposed to underpin or otherwise strengthen or safeguard the foundations of the building or structure of the adjoining owner.

Section 6(5)

In order to exercise his rights the building owner must serve an appropriate notice one month before he proposes to do any work.

The adjoining owner is entitled to receive from the building owner the notice and the building owner's intentions on whether he intends to carry out any strengthening or safeguarding works. As mentioned above, the adjoining owner should then take professional advice and normally the cost of this will be met by the building owner.

The notice to be valid has to be carefully drawn up with all the required information; see s.6(6).

(6) The notice referred to in subsection (5) shall be accompanied by plans and sections showing:–

(a) the site and depth of any excavation the building owner proposed to make;
(b) if he proposed to erect a building or structure, its site.

Section 6(6)

To be valid the notice in s.6(5) has to be accompanied by plans showing the relationship of the buildings and the related depths of proposed excavation, foundations and any other relevant information.

The plans/sections must show the proposed works and the adjoining owners building/excavation proposals.

If this information is not shown the notice will be invalid.

(7) If an owner on whom a notice referred to in subsection (5) has been served does not serve a notice indicating his consent to it within the period of fourteen days beginning with the day on which the notice referred to in subsection (5) was served, he shall be deemed to have dissented from the notice and a dispute shall be deemed to have arisen between the parties.

Section 6(7)

Unless the adjoining owner consents in writing he is deemed to have dissented.

He can however, subsequently agree or he can write back and say he does not agree.

If he does not respond (a deemed dispute) or disagrees (a dispute) the procedures under s.10 for resolving disputes (deemed or actual) come into force.

(8) The notice referred to in subsection (5) shall cease to have effect if the work to which the notice relates–

(a) has not begun within the period of twelve months beginning with the day on which the notice was served; and
(b) is not prosecuted with due diligence.

Section 6(8)
The notice will become invalid after 12 months or if the matter is not pursued with reasonable expedition. This provision is reasonable giving an adjoining owner should not be left in uncertainty.

(9) On completion of any work executed in pursuance of this section the building owner shall if so requested by the adjoining owner supply him with particulars including plans and sections of the work.

Section 6(9)
On request an adjoining owner is entitled to a set of as built drawings from the building owner.

Practice Note
In construction work carried out under the Health & Safety at Work Act it is now common practice to ensure a 'file' on the work is prepared and made available to the building owners.

(10) Nothing in this section shall relieve the building owner from any liability to which he would otherwise be subject for injury to any adjoining owner or any adjoining occupier by reason of work executed by him.

Section 6(10)
The building owner (with or without the specific consent of the adjoining owner), remains strictly liable for any damage he may cause and just because he has the right it does not exonerate him from his liabilities.

Practice Note
The potential for doing damage by excavation and working at a lower level than an adjoining property cannot be overstated. Careful pre planning and advice is needed to ensure the adjoining owners premises are properly safeguarded.

The need to record the condition of the adjoining owners premises and land are extremely important in these circumstances.

Rights Etc.

Compensation etc.

7.–(1) A building owner shall not exercise any right conferred on him by this Act in such a manner or at such time as to cause unnecessary inconvenience to any adjoining owner or to any adjoining occupier.

Section 7(1)

The operative word is unnecessary because any building work is likely to cause some inconvenience. If the work is properly pre-planned and the construction methods are the normal way of doing the work the building owner will be acting reasonably.

Under the terms of the Act it is possible to control how and when the work (which is subject of the Act) can be carried out. There are other limitations on working hours/conditions and the writer is aware of:

(1) Large estates controlling working methods and times by regulations under estate clauses in leases.

(2) Control of Pollution Act notices served by local authorities, this can restrict a working day to 6 or 4 hours.

(3) Town & Country Planning Acts for general working hours.

If the building owner has the option of a quick noisy way of doing the work or a slow quiet way he is really bound to choose the latter. This is especially true if the former will cause unnecessary inconvenience.

Some owners have particularly noise sensitive businesses; e.g. sound recording studios. In these circumstances a reasonable solution to noise and working hours can be difficult to find.

(2) The building owner shall compensate any adjoining owner and any adjoining occupier for any loss or damage which may result to any of them by reason of any work executed in pursuance of this Act.

Section 7(2)

The building owner has to compensate any adjoining owner for loss or damage caused and the compensation can take different forms depending on the type of damage. In the event of physical damage the building owner can do the work or if the adjoining owner prefers he can be paid under s.11 (8) by the building owner.

Any claim for financial loss has to be a direct consequence of the work carried out under the Act.

(3) Where a building owner is exercising any right conferred on him by this Act lays open any part of the adjoining land or building he shall at his own expense make and maintain so long as may be necessary a proper hoarding, shoring or fans or temporary construction for the protection of the adjoining land or building and the security of any adjoining occupier.

Section 7(3)
When the building owner lays open any adjoining owners land or building he has to hoard off/protect the adjoining land and building. He also has the responsibility of maintaining an adjoining owners security.

The requirement of this section are the embodiment of good neighbourly behaviour but the detail of the provisions to be made will entirely depend on the circumstances of the case.

The writer is aware of scaffold alarms, security devices and intruder alarms being provided to protect adjoining owners.

The costs of demolishing and rebuilding a party wall with the associated compensation and ancillary protection works in most cases will be prohibitive. Work to essential public buildings and prestige properties could be an exception. But beware of the cost!

(4) Nothing in this Act shall authorise the building owner to place special foundations on land of an adjoining owner without his previous consent in writing.

Section 7(4)
Special foundations are defined in section 20 and it effectively means foundations including an assembly of beams or rods.

Only with the specific agreement of an adjoining owner can they be placed on an adjoining owners land.

To subsequently alter or remove special foundations under the provisions of the Act will be expensive. Therefore it is normally only sensible to agree to such a proposition if there is no possibility of having to alter or remove them.

(5) Any works executed in pursuance of this Act shall–

(a) comply with the provisions of statutory requirements; and
(b) be executed in accordance with such plans, sections and particulars as may be agreed between the owners or in the event of dispute determined in accordance with section 10;

and no deviation shall be made from those plans, sections and particulars except such as may be agreed between the owners (or surveyors acting on their behalf) or in the vent of dispute determined in accordance with section 10.

Section 7(5)
All work carried out under the Act must comply with statutory requirements and in accordance with the plans/details agreed between the owners/or in accordance with S.10.

No deviations to the detail of these agreed documents can be made except by agreement.

Rights of entry

8.–(1) A building owner, his servants, agents and workmen may during usual working hours enter and remain on any land or premises for the purpose of executing any work in pursuance of this Act and may remove any furniture or fittings or take any other action necessary for that purpose.

Section 8(1)

This section of the Act gives a building owner the right to go onto the adjoining owners land to carry out necessary work.

The hours that may be worked are described as the 'usual' hours.

This section allows building owner to erect scaffold to carry out the works and normally this should only remain in place while the 'Act' works are carried out. This can give rise to difficulties for example when a building owner constructs a party wall with a lean-to roof against it. The construction of the new party wall using the scaffold on the adjoining owners land will be authorised but the roof may not be.

(2) If the premises are closed, the building owner, his agents and workmen may, if accompanied by a constable or other police officer, break open any fences or doors in order to enter the premises.

Section 8(2)

If the adjoining owner is absent or uncooperative this right exists to gain access into an adjoining owners premises to carry out the works.

However, this right must be considered only as a last resort measure. From experience it can only be exercised if the police solicitor is convinced that there is no other option and only if he is convinced the proper procedures have been followed. In the one case the writer has been involved with under this section the proposed use of the section was sufficient to open the door and persuade an irrationally obstinate adjoining owner to co-operate.

(3) No land or premises may be entered by any person under subsection (1) unless the building owner serves on the owner and the occupier of the land or premises:–

(a) in case of emergency, such notice of the intention to enter as may be reasonably practicable;

(b) in any other case, such notice of the intention to enter as complies with subsection (4).

Section 8(3)

To enter the land of another is a right which has to be implemented reasonably and seen to be operated in such a manner. Normally, fourteen days notice has to be given for routine matters with the exception of emergencies where the notice must be reasonably practicable.

(4) Notice complies with this subsection if it is served in a period of not less than fourteen days ending with the day of the proposed entry.

Section 8(4)
As noted above reasonable notice for routine matters is deemed to be fourteen days.

(5) A surveyor appointed or selected under section 10 may during usual working hours enter and remain on any land or premises for the purpose of carrying out the object for which he is appointed or selected.

Section 8(5)
The rights of surveyors to enter the land of either owner is given by this section. While the right is given, it is only courteous and reasonable to inform owners of the intended visits or inspections, and the surveyor can only use the visit for his purposes for which he was appointed. Under s.8(6) there is a timetable for giving notice.

(6) No land or premises may be entered by a surveyor under subsection (5) unless the building owner who is a party to the dispute concerned serves on the owner and the occupier of the land or premises:–

(a) in case of emergency, such notice of the intention to enter as may be reasonably practicable;

(b) in any other case, such notice of the intention to enter as compiles with subsection (4).

Section 8(6)
As with workmen and others in section s.8(3) above, fourteen days notice has to be given for a surveyor to enter the land of an adjoining owner.

Easements

(9) Nothing in this Act shall:–

(a) authorise any interference with an easement of light or other easements in or relating to a party wall, or

(b) prejudicially or restore any right or other thing in or connected with a party wall in case of the party wall being pulled down or rebuilt.

Section 9
The Act does not authorise interference with any existing easement and it particularly refers to rights of light.

As a result of subsection (b) an owner has the right to retain/restore/preserve any other feature of a party wall which is being pulled down or altered.

This clause does however, present potential conflict with s.2. In particular s.2(2)h permits a building owner to cut off an overhanging eaves subject to making good any damage.

In the writer view s.2 rights have precedence over this section 9 limitation.

The rights to light issue can lead to considerable difficulty with party wall matters and any Award or agreement made in such circumstances should specifically mention/refer to an un-concluded issue in this respect.

The resolution of Disputes

Section 10
The resolution of disputes procedure under the Act closely follows the previous party wall legislation and covers all eventualities. Perhaps the most proactive provisions of the Act in this respect are available where an adjoining owner deliberately does nothing.

This behaviour will not frustrate the Act as can be seen in s.10(4)(a)&(b). The writer has tried unsuccessfully to produce a flow chart for this section because there are so many permutations.

Resolution of Disputes

10.–(1) Where a dispute arises or is deemed to have arisen between a building owner and an adjoining owner in respect of any matter connected with any work to which this Act relates either:–

(a) both parties shall concur in the appointment of one surveyor (in this section referred to a an "agreed surveyor"); or

(b) each party shall appoint a surveyor and the two surveyors so appointed shall forthwith select a third surveyor (all of whom are in this section referred to as "the three surveyors").

Section 10(1)
Following service of a notice, a dispute can arise from two sets of circumstances:–

(a) an adjoining owner writes to say he objects to the proposed works.

(b) an adjoining owner does nothing/does not respond within the time limits set down. This is a deemed dispute.

Whether the dispute is actual or deemed the parties can either:–

(a) appoint one surveyor to act for both parties – he becomes the agreed surveyor.

(b) each appoint a surveyor. These two surveyors then have to appoint a third surveyor.

The role of the third surveyor is detailed below but his role is to arbitrate and advise the 'two surveyors' in the event of a dispute.

From experience, the writer has found that the appointment of a single or 'agreed' surveyor works well where there are relatively minor works to be carried out and there are no real contentious items. It is a natural reaction for an owner to want his own surveyor in difficult situations. However, the surveyor once appointed has a responsibility to administer the Act objectively and not to be at the beck and call of his owner who sometimes may wish to use the Act as a tool of frustration. In such circumstances, a surveyor will need tact, professionalism, objectivity and resolution.

(2) All appointments and selections made under this section shall be in writing and shall not be rescinded by either party.

Section 10(2)
A surveyor has to be appointed in writing for his appointment to be effective/binding/legal. However, once appointed in writing, an owner cannot rescind/cancel the appointment.

This comes as a surprise to most laymen and an owner cannot dismiss a surveyor because he does not like what is happening.

An owner can challenge any agreement/Award made by his surveyor but he has to do so under s.10(7) by appeal to the County Court. Therefore, if an owner has been kept informed throughout the negotiations between the surveyors decides to go to court, he has to be very clear about why he is dissatisfied. The courts take a dim view of mindless prevarication.

(3) If an agreed surveyor:–

(a) refuses to act;
(b) neglects to act for a period of ten days beginning with the day on which either party serves a request on him;
(c) dies before the dispute is settled; or
(d) becomes or deems himself incapable of acting, the proceedings for settling such dispute shall begin *de novo*.

Section 10(3)
If an agreed surveyor refuses fails or cannot act the procedures for selecting a surveyor/surveyors will begin anew.

Examples of such circumstances where a surveyor cannot act include pressure of work, illness or absence.

The failure to act cannot therefore frustrate the purposes of the Act for very long.

(4) If either party to the dispute:–

(a) refuses to appoint a surveyor under subsection (1)(b), or
(b) neglects to appoint a surveyor under subsection (1)(b) for a period of ten days beginning with the day on which the other party serves a request on him, the other party may make the appointment on his behalf.

Section 10(4)
This section gives the right to the other party to appoint a surveyor in the case of refusal or neglect.

Therefore, an owner cannot frustrate the procedure. If an owner does invoke this section, it is important he is seen to appoint an objective impartial person to act as a surveyor.

(5) If, before the dispute is settled, a surveyor appointed under paragraph (b) of subsection (1) by a party to the dispute dies, or becomes or deems himself incapable of acting, the party who appointed him may appoint another surveyor in his place with the same power and authority.

Section 10(5)
An owner can replace his surveyor but only if he dies, becomes incapable of acting or deems himself incapable. An owner can exert various sorts of pressure on a surveyor in the event of dissatisfaction, but he cannot rescind his appointment.

(6) If a surveyor:–

(a) appointed under paragraph (b) of subsection (1) by a party to the dispute; or
(b) appointed under subsection (4) or 5),

refuses to act effectively, the surveyor of the other party may proceed to act *ex parte* and anything so done by him shall be as effectual as if he had been an agreed surveyor.

Section 10(6)
In a case where there are two surveyors appointed (one for each party) a surveyor who refuses to act effectively, will be bypassed by this section because the other surveyor can proceed by himself. Once invoked this allows the remaining surveyor to act as agreed surveyor under s.10(1)(a). To invoke this ex parte *procedure is a high risk stategy and in the event of an Award being challenged in the Courts, the surveyor who invoked the procedure would have to prove conclusively that he had acted impartially.*

The word 'effectively' is open to interpretation and the writer is not aware of any instance of this clause being used.

(7) If a surveyor:–

(a) appointed under paragraph (b) of subsection (1) by a party to the dispute; or
(b) appointed under subsection (4) or (5),

neglects to act effectively for a period of ten days beginning with the day on which either party or the surveyor of the other party serves a request on him, the surveyor of the other party may proceed at act *ex parte* in respect of the subject matter of the request and anything so done by him shall be as effectual as if he had been an agreed surveyor.

Section 10(7)
This section places a time constraint on the surveyor to act effectively and gives him ten days to get his act together.

Usually, a notice to this effect brings a positive response and the matter proceeds.

(8) If either surveyor appointed under subsection 1(b) by a party to the dispute refuses to select a third surveyor under subsection (1) or (9), or neglects to do so for a period of ten days beginning with the day on which the other surveyor serves a request on him:–

(a) the appointing officer; or
(b) in cases where the relevant appointing officer or his employer is a party to the dispute, the Secretary of State,

may on the application of either surveyor select a third surveyor who shall have the same power and authority as if he had been selected under subsection (1) or subsection (9).

Section 10(8)
If either of the two surveyors refuse or neglect to appoint a third surveyor, this clause provides the ability to do so.

The appointing officer will normally be a Senior Building Control Officer.

Again, the principal behind these provisions is to ensure that progress can be made.

(9) If a third surveyor selected under subsection (1)(b):–

(a) refuses to act;
(b) neglects to act for a period of ten days beginning with the day on which either party or the surveyor appointed by either party serves a request on him; or
(c) dies, or becomes or deem himself incapable of acting, before the dispute is settled,

the other two of the three surveyors shall forthwith select another surveyor in his place with the same power and authority.

Section 10(9)
This section gives two of the three surveyors the power to select or a new third surveyor if the third surveyor cannot or will not act.

The writer has had cause to use this section and the third surveyor did not contest his removal having been given a ten day opportunity.

(10) The agreed surveyor or as the case may be, the three surveyors or any two of them shall settle by award any matter:–

(a) Which is connected with any work to which this Act relates and,
(b) which is an dispute between the building owner and the adjoining owner.

Section 10(10)
The word 'Award' means a written signed document which is delivered to the respective owners. Normally, the agreed surveyor or the two surveyors conclude the Award in a reasonable period having inspected the premises/properties and having informed their owners of the deliberations. The surveyor(s) only have the power to determine matters which are the subject of the Act.

(11) Either of the parties or either of the surveyors appointed by the parties may call upon the third surveyor selected in pursuance of this section to determine the disputed matters and he shall make the necessary Award.

Section 10(11)
If for any reason the two owners or surveyors cannot reach agreement they can call upon the third surveyor to determine the disputed items and issue an Award.

(12) An award may determine:–

(a) the right to execute any work;
(b) the time and manner of executing any work; and
(c) any other matter arising out of or incidental to the dispute including the costs of making the Award;

but any period appointed by the Award for executing any work shall not unless otherwise agreed between the building owner and the adjoining owner being to run until after the expiration of the period prescribed by this Act for service of the notice in respect of which the dispute arises or is deemed to have arisen.

Section 10(12)
The Award should clearly deal with the scope of the work, the timing and the method to be employed. It should also cover all the issues on costs.

However, an Award cannot alter the period prescribed by the Act for service of notices. This can however, be dealt with by specific agreement in writing between the owners.

This clause is wide ranging and most matters can be simply and straight forwardly dealt with by the surveyor(s) and recorded in the Award.

The form an Award takes is not set out in the Act but in the appendix there is a typical example.

(13) The reasonable costs incurred in:–

(a) making or obtaining an Award under this section;
(b) reasonable inspections of work to which the Award relates; and
(c) any other matter arising out of the dispute,

shall be paid by such of the parties as the surveyor or surveyors making the Award determine.

Section 10(13)
The surveyors or agreed surveyor making the Award determine who shall bear the costs of making the Award inspections and any matter arising from the dispute.

Normally, the party ***initiating*** *the procedures meet the costs.*

Costs in making Awards normally cover surveyor's fees but can include engineer's fees for both parties to enable the surveyor to be confident that the agreed works are not prejudicial to the various buildings or structures.

In the event of disagreement on the application or levels of costs/fees in this section between two surveyors, the third surveyor should be called upon to decide.

(14) Where the surveyors appointed by the parties make an Award the surveyors shall serve it forthwith on the parties.

Section 10(14)
The surveyors must serve the Award as soon as they have signed it. Normally, a surveyor sends the signed Award to his owner on the same day that it is completed.

(15) Where an Award is made by the third surveyor:–

(a) he shall, after payment of the costs of the Award, serve it forthwith on the parties or their appointed surveyors; and
(b) if it is served on their appointed surveyors, they shall serve it forthwith on the parties.

> **Section 10(15)**
> *Where a third surveyor makes an Award, he must deliver it to the owners/surveyors as soon as his fee has been paid.*

(16) The Award shall be conclusive and shall not except as provided by this section be questioned in any court.

> **Section 10(16)**
> *The Award, once signed and delivered is the document / agreement which deals with dispute/deemed dispute.*
>
> *It can only be questioned as set out in subsection 10(17) below.*

(17) Either of the parties to the dispute may, within the period of fourteen days, beginning with the day on which an Award made under this section is served on him, appeal to the county court against the Award and the county court may:–

(a) rescind the Award or modify it in such manner as the court thinks fit; and
(b) make such order as to costs as the court thinks fit.

> **Section 10(17)**
> *It either party to the Award is not satisfied with the Award terms, they may appeal to the County Court within the fourteen days of the date on which the Award has been served on him. It is therefore essential the Awards are delivered promptly and the owners are made aware of their rights. If the matter has been contentious, a surveyor should specifically tell his owner that he is due to issue the Award so the owner may be prepared.*
>
> *The County Court can rescind, modify or uphold an Award.*

Expenses

11.–(1) Except as provided under this section expenses of work under this Act shall be defrayed by the building owner.

(2) Any dispute as to responsibility for expenses shall be settled as provided in section 10.

> **Section 11(1) & (2)**
> *The building owner having* ***instigated*** *the procedures is normally responsible for the costs.*
>
> *If there is a dispute on expenses/costs the resolution of dispute procedure in s.10 will be implemented.*

(3) An expense mentioned in section 1(3)(b) shall be defrayed as there mentioned.

> **Section 11(3)**
> *This section refers to the costs of building a party wall or party fence wall. The division of costs is made according to the use each party makes of the wall.*
>
> *In the case of a party fence wall a normal arrangement would be an equal division. However, to get to this situation both parties must agree to the building of the party structure and its characteristics. This does not happen very often in practice.*

(4) Where work is carried out in exercise of the right mentioned in section 2(2)(a), and the work is necessary on account of defect or want of repair of the structure or wall concerned, the expenses shall be defrayed by the building owner and the adjoining owner in such proportion as has regard to:–

(a) the use which the owners respectively make or may make of the structure or wall concerned; and
(b) responsibility for the defect or want of repair concerned, if more than one owner makes of the structure or wall concerned.

> **Section 11(4)**
> *Section 2(2)(a) applies to cases where a Party Structure or Building Owner Wall against a structure needs to be raised, thickened or underpinned due to disrepair.*
>
> *The costs are then apportioned according to the use of the wall or the responsibility for the defect.*
>
> *This section is designed to cover situations where an innocent party is not made to pay for costs to rectify a situation which is not of his making.*

(5) Where work is carried out in exercise of the light mentioned in section 2(2)(b) the expenses shall be defrayed by the building owner and the adjoining owner in such proportion as has regard to:–

(a) the use which the owners respectively make or may make of the structure or wall concerned; and
(b) responsibility for the defect or want of repair concerned, if more than one owner makes use of the structure or wall concerned.

Section 11(5)

Section 2(2)(b) involves repairs, demolition and rebuild of a party structure.

The cost apportionment between owners is made according to:–

(a) use.

(b) responsibility of defect or want of repair.

The apportionment of costs in such cases is always dependant on the circumstances and can be very difficult to resolve.

(6) Where the adjoining premises are laid open in exercise of the right mentioned in section 2(2)(e) a fair allowance in respect of disturbance and inconvenience shall be paid by the building owner to the adjoining owner or occupier.

Section 11(6)

This section is designed to compensate an adjoining owner for inconvenience and disturbance when their premises, gardens etc. are laid open.

The costs involving laying open a house will be considerable and should be avoided if at all possible. A carefully designed hoarding in a garden can effectively reduce such disturbance/inconvenience to a nominal sum when constructing a boundary wall.

(7) Where a building owner proposes to reduce the height of a party wall or party fence wall under section 2(2)(m) the adjoining owner may serve a counter notice under section 4 requiring the building owner to maintain the existing height of the wall and in such case, the adjoining owner shall pay to the building owner a due proportion of the cost of the wall so far as it exceeds:–

(a) two metres in height; or
(b) the height currently enclosed upon by the building of the adjoining owner.

Section 11(7)

Where it is proposed to reduce the party wall or party fence wall in height, an adjoining owner can serve a counter notice saying he wishes to maintain the present height.

If the counter notice is served the adjoining owner has to pay the building owner a percentage of the costs so far as it exceeds 2 metres or the height of current enclosure.

Agreeing such costs is generally difficult.

(8) Where the building owner is required to make good damage under this Act the adjoining owner has a right to require that the expenses of such making good be determined in accordance with section 10 and paid to him in lieu of the carrying out of work to make the damage good.

Section 11(8)
The building owner has a strict obligation to make good any damage. However, if damage is caused the adjoining owner has the right to ask for a monetary payment in lieu. This is sound physiology because if the damage arises out of lack of care, the last thing an adjoining owner will want is the building owners builder coming to put right the damage.

To resolve such issues, surveyors often ask for several quotations for the reinstatement works, including a quote from the building owner's contractor.

If there is dispute as to the quantity of the claim, the s.10 procedures would be followed.

(9) Where:–

(a) works are carried out, and
(b) some of the works are carried out at the request of the adjoining owner or in pursuance of a requirement made by him,

he shall defray the expenses of carrying out the works requested or required by him.

Section 11(9)
If an adjoining owner asks for some works to be carried out under a counter notice, he has to pay for them. Normally, the additional works would be costed prior to work commencing, the costs would be agreed and the Award would include the provisions.

(10) Where:–

(a) consent in writing has been given to the construction of special foundations on land of an adjoining owner; and
(b) the adjoining owner erects any building or structure and its cost is found to be increased by reason of the existence of the said foundations,

the owner of the building to which the said foundations belong shall, on receiving an account with any necessary invoices and other supporting documents within the period of two months beginning with the day of the completion of the work by the adjoining owner, repay to the adjoining owner so much of the cost as is due to the existence of the said foundations.

Section 11(10)
If special foundations are constructed by a building owner (and only with specific consent) and an adjoining owner costs of construction are increased by reason of the special foundations the adjoining owner can claim payment for the additional cost from the building owner.

The existence of special foundations can therefore present considerable problems for either party and as a general rule it is better to treat them as a matter of last resort.

(11) Where use is subsequently made by the adjoining owner of work carried out solely at the expense of the building owner the adjoining owner shall pay a due proportion of the expenses incurred by the building owner in carrying out that work; and for this purpose he shall be taken to have incurred expenses calculated by reference to what the cost of the work would be if it were carried out at the time where that subsequent use is made.

Section 11(11)
If an owner subsequently uses a section of the party wall that he has not paid for previously, he has to pay for it (a proper share) at the prevailing rates for work when he uses it.

Payment is normally paid to the freeholder of the property unless there is a lease provision which specifically states otherwise.

Security for Expenses

12.–(1) An adjoining owner may serve a notice requiring the building owner before he begins any work in the exercise of the rights conferred by this Act to give such security as may be agreed between the owners or in the event of dispute determined in accordance with section 10.

Section 12(1)
When the cost of the work is high or where there may be some doubt on the financial standing of the building owner the adjoining owner can serve a notice requiring security to be given.

The security is normally provided by a bank account being set up in the names of the three surveyors and the money released on the signatures of any two. Any interest on the account monies is paid to the building owner.

(2) Where:–

(a) in the exercise of the rights conferred by this Act an adjoining owner requires the building owner to carry out any work the expenses of which are to be defrayed in whole or in party by the adjoining owner, or
(b) an adjoining owner serves a notice on the building owner under subsection (1),

the building owner may before beginning the work to which the requirement or notice relates serve a notice on the adjoining owner requiring him to give such security as may be agreed between the owners or in the event of dispute determined in accordance with section 10.

> **Section 12(2)**
> *When the building owner is asked to carry additional works by the adjoining owner, he may by notice, require security for expense from the adjoining owner.*

(3) If within the period of one month beginning with:–

(a) the day on which a notice is served under subsection (2); or
(b) in the event of dispute, the date of determination by the surveyor or surveyors,

the adjoining owner does not comply with the notice of the determination, the requirement or notice by him to which the building owner's notice under that subsection relates shall cease to have effect.

> **Section 12(3)**
> *If an adjoining owner does not comply with a request for security or an Award of it, his request for additional works will lapse.*
>
> *After the lapse of one month the building owner is no longer under an obligation to carry out the works.*
>
> *The period of one month is reasonable given the fact that the building owner is likely to be held up in these circumstances.*

Account for work carried out

13.–(1) Within the period of two months beginning with the day of the completion of any work executed by a building owner of which the expenses are to be wholly or partially defrayed by an adjoining owner in accordance with section 11 the building owner shall serve on the adjoining owner an account in writing showing:–

(a) particulars and expenses of the work; and
(b) any deductions to which the adjoining owner or any other person is entitled in respect of old materials and otherwise;

and in preparing the account the work shall be estimated and valued at fair average rates and prices according to the nature of the work, the locality and the cost of labour and materials prevailing at the time when the work is executed.

Section 13(1)
This section sets out the accounting period and details to be provided when a building owner carries out work wholly or partially paid for by the adjoining owner. Often these costs are estimated prior to work commencing and any variations agreed as the work proceeds so there are no nasty shocks of a financial nature.

It is prudent to set out in the Award the total costs, the shares each party will bear and how and when the costs will be paid. All this will eliminate doubt and potential difficulty.

(2) Within the period of one month beginning with the day of service of the said account the adjoining owner may serve on the building owner a notice stating any objection he may have thereto and thereupon a dispute shall be deemed to have arisen between the parties.

(3) If within that period of one month the adjoining owner does not serve notice under subsection (2) he shall be deemed to have no objection to the account.

Section 13(2) & (3)
An adjoining owner can object to the statement of account within one month. If he does a dispute has arisen and it will have to be resolved under s.10.

If there is no objection within one month, he has deemed to have no objection.

As noted above, it is better to pre-empt these problems by setting out the cost contributions in the Award.

Settlement of Account

14.–(1) All expenses to be defrayed by an adjoining owner in accordance with an account served under section 13 shall be paid by the adjoining owner.

(2) until an adjoining owner pays to the building owner such expenses as aforesaid the property in any works executed under this Act to which the expenses relate shall be vested solely in the building owner.

Section 14(1) & (2)
The adjoining owner has to pay for the works carried out for him.

Until he has paid the building owner, he retains ownership but this is often of little value.

Miscellaneous

15.–(1) A notice or other document required or authorised to be served under this Act may be served on a person:–

(a) by delivering it to him in person;
(b) by sending it by post to him at his usual or last known residence or place of business in the United Kingdom; or
(c) in the case of body corporate, by delivering it to the secretary or clerk of the body corporate at its registered or principal office or sending it by post to the secretary or clerk of that body corporate at that office.

> **Section 15(1)**
> *These clauses set out the requirements for delivery of notices. If in doubt, serve the notice by hand and introduce yourself to the adjoining owner. Personal contact in the writer's experience will ease the passage of the whole process.*

(2) In the case of a notice or other document required or authorised to be served under this Act on a person as owner of premises, it may alternatively be served by:–

(a) addressing it "the owner" of the premises (naming them), and
(b) delivering it to a person on the premises or, if no person to whom it can be delivered is found there, fixing it to a conspicuous part of the premises.

> **Section 15(2)**
> *Where the adjoining owner's name is not known, it can be served by addressing to "The Owner" and including the address. Delivery can be achieved by giving it to a person on the premises.*
>
> *If there are no persons on site, fix the notice to the front door. It is often prudent to photograph the affixed notice to prove service should the need arise.*

Offences

16.–(1) If:–

(a) an occupier of land or premises refuses to permit a person to do anything which he is entitled to do with regard to the land or premises under section 8(1) or (5); and
(b) the occupier knows or has reasonable cause to believe that the person is so entitled,

the occupier is guilty of an offence.

Section 16(1)
It is a crime to prevent access to someone authorised to enter a building land etc. when they have the right to do so under s.8.

Whether the occupier knows or has reasonable cause to know can only be established by the facts of the case.

16.–(2) If:-

(a) a person hinders or obstructs a person in attempting to do anything which he is entitled to do so with regard to land or premises under section 8(1) or (5); and
(b) the first mentioned person knows or has reasonable cause to believe that the other person is so entitled, the first mentioned person is guilty of an offence.

Section 16(2)
An offence is committed if a person hinders or obstructs a person entitled to enter land or buildings under s.8(1) or (5).

In a development where there are numerous adjoining owners, there are instances where this has occurred inadvertently. In the writer's experience a letter written in clear terms with copies to all parties normally prevents misunderstandings.

(3) A person guilty of an offence under subsection (1) or (2) is liable on summary conviction to a fine an amount not exceeding level 3 on the standard scale.

Section 16(3)
This clause sets the fines to a standard scale. If the scale changes with time, so do the fines.

The court for dealing with contraventions of the Act is the court of primary criminal jurisdiction, i.e. the 'Magistrates Court'.

Recovery of sums

17. Any sum payable in pursuance of this Act (otherwise than by way of fine) shall be recoverable summarily as a civil debt.

Section 17
In the event of non payment, an owner can recover the sums due as a civil debt.

Exception in the case of Temples etc

18.–(1) This Act shall not apply to land which is situated in inner London and in which there is an interest belonging to:–

(a) the Honourable Society of the Inner Temple,
(b) the Honourable Society of the Middle Temple,
(c) the Honourable Society of Lincoln' Inn, or
(d) the Honourable Society of Gray's Inn.

(2) the reference in subsection (1) to inner London is to Greater London other than the outer London boroughs.

> **Section 18(1) & (2)**
> *The Inns of Court were exempt from the previous Acts and retain their exemption.*
>
> *Inner London is defined in (2) because the old LCC area (Inner London) is not defined anywhere else in the Act.*

The Crown

19.–(1) This Act shall apply to land in which there is:–
(a) an interest belonging to Her Majesty in right of the Crown,
(b) an interest belonging to a government department,
or
(c) an interest held on trust for Her Majesty for the purpose of any such department.

(2) This Act shall apply to:–
(a) land which is vested in, but not occupied by Her Majesty in right of the Duchy of Lancaster.
(b) land which is vested in, but not occupied by the possessor for the time being of the Duchy of Cornwall.

> **Section 19(1) & (2)**
> *The Act applies to the Crown except if the property is occupied by Her Majesty in the right of the Duchy of Lancaster or by the possessor of the Duchy of Cornwall.*

Interpretation

20. In this Act, unless the context otherwise requires, the following expressions have the meanings hereby respectively assigned to them:–

> *s.20 contains the definitions of the terms used regularly throughout the Act.*

Adjoining owner/adjoining occupier

"adjoining owner" and "adjoining occupier" respectively mean any owner and any occupier of land, buildings, storeys or rooms adjoining those of the building owner and for the purposes only of section 6 within the distances specified in that section;

Section 20 adjoining owner/adjoining occupier
It is important to release that there may be many adjoining owners/occupiers within one building and the definition of owner below is critical to the reasonable application of the Act and its safeguards for adjoining rights.

Appointing Officer

"appointing officer" means the person appointed under this Act by the local authority to make such appointments as are required under section 10(8);

Section 20 appointing officer
If two surveyors cannot agree to selection of the third surveyor, then they can refer to the local authority. Normally, this person will be within the Building Regulation department.

"building owner" means an owner of land who is desirous of exercising rights under this Act;

Section 20 building owner
A building owner is the owner of the land who wishes to exercise his rights.

An building owner can be a company, trust, person or any legal entity owning an interest in land. The precise owner of the land must be included in the Notices for them to be valid.

"foundation", in relation to a wall, means the solid ground or artificially formed support resting on solid ground on which the wall rests;

Section 20 foundation
Foundations include the ground under the wall / walls and encompass rafts, beams, piles and typical concrete strips.

Traditional building methods include brick offsets for foundations with metal hoops built in. In the writer's experience the metal hoops are not "special foundations".

"owner" includes:–

(a) a person in receipt of, or entitled to receive, the whole or part of the rents or profits of land;

(b) a person in possession of land, otherwise than as a mortgagee or as a tenant from year to year or for a lesser term or as a tenant at will;

(c) a purchaser of an interest in land under a contract for purchase or under an agreement for a lease, otherwise than under an agreement for a tenancy from year to year or for a lessor term;

Section 20 owner

The definition of owner needs careful study because it includes persons who would normally not meet the layman's perception of owner. It includes freeholders, lessees with a term of more than one year and a purchaser with a contract or agreement for lease for a term of one year.

Therefore, in a building there can be numerous owners and subject to meeting the requirements of this definition, they are all entitled to a notice and to have their interests safeguarded.

"party fence wall" means a wall (not being part of a building) which stands on lands of different owners and is used or constructed to be used for separating such adjoining lands, but does not include a wall constructed on the land of one owner the artificially formed support of which projects into the land of another owner;

Section 20 party fence wall

In simple terms, a party fence wall is a garden wall built astride / over the boundary but it does not include any wall which forms part of a building.

"party structure" means a party wall and also a floor partition or other structure separating buildings or parts of building approached solely by separate staircases or separate entrances.

Section 20 party structure

The party structures definition includes walls, floors and other structure separating buildings or parts of buildings.

This is relevant to maisonettes, blocks of flats, offices where they have separate entrances.

Given the multiplicity of owners the permutations of owners and party structures is considerable.

A party wall has two definitions

"party wall" means:–

(a) a wall which forms part of a building and stands on lands of different owners to a greater extent than the projection of any artificially formed support on which the wall rests; and

(b) so much of a wall not being a wall referred to in paragraph (a) above as separates buildings belonging to different owners;

Section 20 (a) & (b) party wall

(a) This definition is clear and is the usual form of party wall. It is a wall built over/astride the boundary line which can separate buildings, but it must always enclose a building.

(b) In this second part of the definition, the important point is that the wall separates the buildings in different ownerships. The only section of wall that are party walls in this definition are the parts which actually separate buildings.

The notion of a party wall does not follow the location of the boundary in this second pat of the definition.

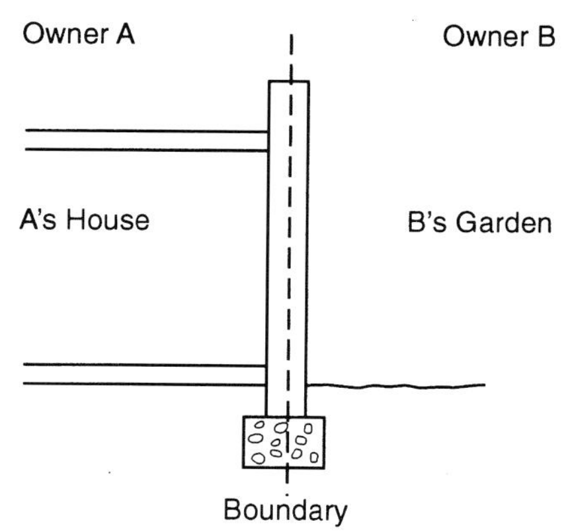

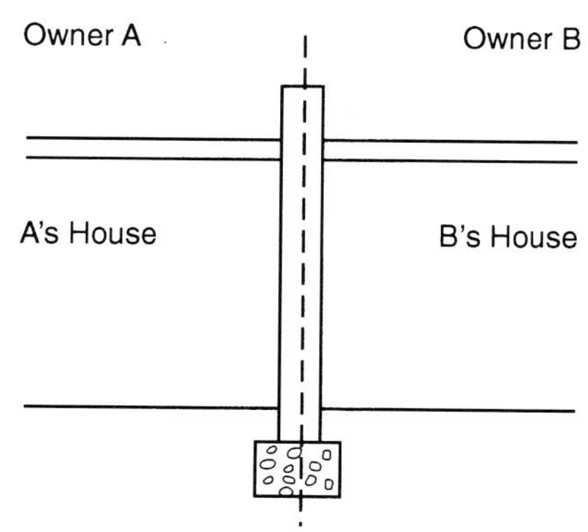

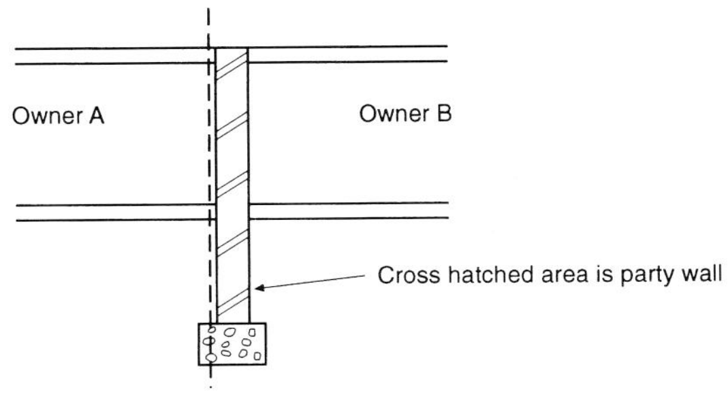

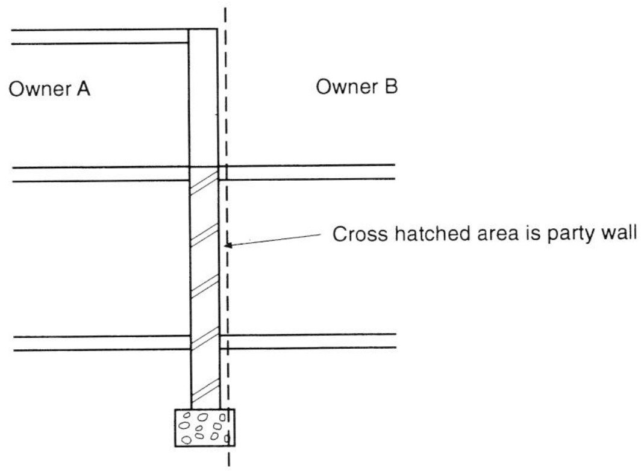

"special foundations" means foundations in which an assemblage of beams or rods is employed for the purpose of distributing any load; and

Section 20 special foundations
This definition of foundations included foundations which are strengthened by rods / beams for distributing loads. This includes steel reinforcing rods, steel beams and reinforcing cages used in pile foundations.

No special foundations can be used unless the express consent of the adjoining owner is given. In practice the use of special foundations should be a last resort.

"surveyor" means any person not being a party to the matter appointed or selected under section 10 to determine disputes in accordance with the procedures set out in this Act.

Section 20 surveyor
A surveyor can be any person other than the owner himself. No qualifications are given, but experience of the Act, building construction, practice and procedures are a prerequisite for a successful holder of the position.

Surveyors, engineers and architects usually perform the functions/roles under the Act.

Other statutory provisions

21.–(1) The Secretary of State may by order amend or repeal any provision of a private or local Act passed before or in the same session as this Act, if it appears to him necessary or expedient to do so in consequence of this Act.

(2) an order under subsection (1) may:–

(a) contain such savings or transitional provisions as the Secretary of State think fit;
(b) make different provision for different purposes.

(3) The power to make an order under subsection (1) shall be exercisable by statutory instrument subject to annulment in pursuance of a resolution of either House of Parliament.

> **Section 21**
> *Where there is an potential clash with local or private Acts the relevant parts can be amended, replaced etc.*

Short title, commencement and extent

22.–(1) This Act may be cited as the Party Wall etc. Act 1996.

(2) This Act shall come into force in accordance with provision made by the Secretary of State by order made by statutory instrument.

(3) An order under subsection (2) may:–

(a) contain such savings or transitional provisions as the Secretary of State thinks fit;
(b) make different provision for different purposes.

(4) This Act extends to England and Wales only.

> **Section 22**
> *These are self explanatory general provisions and define the application of the Act. The Acts apply to England and Wales only. Please refer to the excluded areas in s.18(1).*

A guide to the Act

Points to be considered when using the Act as a Building Owner

(1) Who precisely is the owner. The owner must serve the notices or authorise his surveyor in writing to serve the notices.

See section 3 for notices.

(2) What work is intended

The notices to be valid have to set out the information required and present it as detailed by the Act – see s.3(1)(a)(b)&(c). The rights contained in the Act are set out in section 1 and 2. The notice/s to be valid have to conform to time periods laid down – see s.3(2)(a)&(b).

Where work is intended adjacent to adjoining owners ensure that notices under sections 6(1) and 6(2) are accompanied by the correct information regarding plans sections showing the site, depths of excavation and proposed works.

(3) Adjoining Owners

Visit the adjoining properties and establish how they are occupied. Find out who is legally to be served with notices as adjoining owners.

Please refer to s.20 for the definitions of adjoining owners.

(4) Serve the notices in accordance with the Act.

(5) Having established what you are proposing to do set out a timetable for progress chasing. Be aware that different works have different timetables; party walls – two months notice, boundary walls – one months notice.

(6) Following service of notices, contact adjoining owners and try to persuade the parties where simple matters are involved to either (a) agree the works – see section 3(3)(a) or (b) the appointment of one "agreed surveyor" see section 10(1)(a).

In either case, the building owner should inform his adjoining owner that the building owner is strictly liable for any damage he may do, he does not intend to do any damage and that the adjoining owner may employ a surveyor to protect his interests if he wishes to.

(7) Following service of notice where relatively major works are involved try to persuade adjoining owners to appoint a surveyor and proceed with the matter under section 10.

(8) A building owner/or his surveyor should always try to meet his adjoining owners and explain what works are proposed and their likely impact. Information and personal contact dispel misinformation, rumour and distrust.

Tell your adjoining owners what it is going to be like when work is going on.

(9) Enter into an Award/Agreement under section 10 and publish it to all the owners.

(10) Tell your neighbours/adjoining owners when work will actually start. Awards allow work to proceed, but they do not usually allow an adjoining owner to insist that the works be carried out. Therefore, keep your adjoining owners informed.

(11) During the course of the works, make regular inspections of the adjoining owners premises (with appropriate periods of notice).

(12) In the event of damage be proactive in assessing its extent, impact on your neighbours and likely costs of reinstatement. As owner you are liable under the Act. Inform your agents, contractors, advisers and inform insurers and ensure your adjoining owner is made aware of the circumstances.

Never hope the problem will go away or hide it.

Acting for the London Borough of Camden as adjoining owner's surveyor in early 1970's, I was involved with a redevelopment of a building abutting the Old Town Hall in High Holborn. During demolition of the building owners building, the demolition contractors had an accident with a ball and chain demolition crane. The ball missed a column, swung 10feet or so past it and embedded itself in the party wall. When I inspected an hour or so later, late on a Friday afternoon, the party wall was neatly covered up with a tarpaulin, the demolition contractors had left site and the crane was parked well away from the point of impact. Inside, I found a considerable new bulge in the party wall brickwork and several broken slabs of marble on the floor in the Mayoral Chamber!

The contractors eventually owned up to having caused the damage after I produced an eye witness who in graphic detail, explained that lunchtime working that particular day, had stopped for three hours, but when it restarted, it was somewhat disorientated and inaccurate!

(13) When the work is complete, inspect the premises and sign off the Award assuming that there are no outstanding matters.

(14) Under the Act, an owner may be liable to account for expenses or have to provide as 'built drawings'. These mattes should not be overlooked.

Points to be considered when you are an adjoining owner or adjoining owners surveyor

(1) On receipt of letters/correspondence/notices, check that they are valid. Insist on seeing the letter of appointment for a building owners surveyor to ensure he is entitled to act and serve notices if so instructed etc.

(2) Check the work is authorised by the Act.

(3) Ensure you are appointed to act as an adjoining owners surveyor in writing.

(4) Inspect your owners premises and the building owners and use your experience to establish how the proposed works will impact on your owners building.

(5) Sit down and identify in writing, what you would do/allow for if the roles were reversed.

(6) Assuming the works are permitted by the Act and properly authorised by a valid notice, write a positive letter to the building owner/his surveyor setting out your sensible reasonable requirements in the matter. This is not an exhaustive list but consider:–

6(1) any structural implications – is a structural engineers input necessary; consider on necessary shoring, strapping, bracing, temporary support and associated works.

6(2) the need for any underpinning or safeguarding under section 6 procedures.

6(3) what protection work may be needed. This may be necessary to physically protect your owners building, openings, fireplace openings and external features.

6(4) provision of sheeting out and protection of roofs.

6(5) health and safety considerations.

6(6) compliance with Building Regulations.

6(7) security works to be provided.

6(8) access arrangements.

6(9) jointly inspect and record the condition of your owners building.

(7) When you have all the information, consider the terms of an Award and deal with matters positively.

(8) Consider working hours for works to the party structure and the nature of your owners occupation, business and organisation.

(9) Keep your owner informed of all relevant matters.

(10) Sign the Award and deliver it to your owner as provided for by the Act.

(11) Collect your fees on signature of the Award.

(12) Monitor progress of works by making inspections. Pre-estimate the number and timing of these visits if you can.

(13) Deal with instances of damage as they occur.

(14) On completion complete any procedures required by the Act and sign off the Award.

THREE METRE/SIX METRE NOTICE

PARTY WALL ETC. ACT, 1996 SECTION 6

To: (Adjoining Owner)
of

*I/We (Building Owner)
of

as owner(s) of

which adjoins your premises known as

HEREBY SERVE YOU WITH NOTICE THAT
*Under Section 6(1)
it is intended to build within 3 metres of your building and to a lower level than the bottom of your foundations, by carrying out the works detailed below, after the expiration of one month from the service of this notice.

Or

*Under Section 6(2)
it is intended to build within 6 metres of your building and to a depth as defined in the Act, by carrying out the works detailed below, after the expiration of one month from the service of this notice.

IT *IS/IS NOT PROPOSED TO UNDERPIN OR OTHERWISE STRENGTHEN IN ORDER TO SAFEGUARD THE FOUNDATIONS OF YOUR BUILDING.

**Delete as appropriate*

The accompanying plans and sections show the site and the excavation depth proposed.

The intended works are:

It is intended to commence works *as soon as notice has run/on the
or earlier by agreement.

Under Section 6(7), if you do not consent to the works within 14 days you are deemed to have dissented and a difference is deemed to have arisen. In such case Section 10 of the Act requires that both parties should concur in the appointment of a surveyor or should each appoint one surveyor and in those circumstances *I\we would appoint
Mr
of (address)

Signed (date)
*Authorised to sign
on behalf of (Building Owner)

**Delete as appropriate*

ACKNOWLEDGEMENT OF THREE METRE/SIX METRE NOTICE

PARTY WALL ETC. ACT, 1996 SECTION 6

*I/We
of

having received the notice served
by
of

in respect of

which adjoins *my/our premises known as

*agree to your proposals
or
*dispute the necessity for underpinning or strengthening the foundations of *my\our building
or
*require you to underpin or strengthen the foundations of *my/our building

and a difference having arisen *concur in the appointment of/appoint as a surveyor
Mr
of (address)

Signed (date)
*Authorised to sign
on behalf of (Adjoining Owner)

**Delete as appropriate*

LINE OF JUNCTION NOTICE

PARTY WALL ETC. ACT, 1996 SECTION 1

To: (Adjoining Owner)
of

*I/We (Building Owner)
of

as owner(s) of the land known as

which adjoins your land known as

HEREBY SERVE YOU WITH NOTICE THAT
*Under Section 1(2), subject to your written consent
it is intended to build on the line of junction of the said lands a *party wall/party fence wall.
*Under Section 1(5)
it is intended to build on the line of junction of the said lands a wall wholly on *my/our own land.
*Under Section 1(6)
it is intended to place projecting footings and foundation on your land at *my/our expense.

*Under section7(4) it *is/is not proposed to employ special foundations, which would require your written consent.

**Delete as appropriate*

The proposed works *as shown on the accompanying drawings/are:

It is intended to commence works *after one month/on the
or earlier by agreement.

In the event of matters arising for settlement *I/we would appoint as *my/our surveyor
Mr
of (address)

Signed (date)
*Authorised to sign
on behalf of (Building Owner)

*Delete as appropriate

PARTY STRUCTURE NOTICE

PARTY WALL ETC. ACT, 1996 SECTION 3

To: (Adjoining Owner)
of

*I/We (Building Owner)
of

as owner(s) of

which adjoins your premises known as

HEREBY SERVE YOU WITH NOTICE THAT, IN ACCORDANCE WITH *MY/OUR RIGHTS:
Under Section 2 Sub-section (2), paragraphs ......
And with reference to the ***party structure/party fence wall** separating the above premises, it is intended to carry out the works details below after the expiration of **two months** from service of this notice.

The proposed works are:

It is intended to commence works *as soon as notice has run/on the
or earlier by agreement.

**Delete as appropriate*

Under Section 5, if you do not consent to the works within 14 days you are deemed to have dissented and a difference is deemed to have arisen. In such case Section 10 of the Act requires that both parties should concur in the appointment of a surveyor or should each appoint one surveyor and in those circumstances *I/we would appoint

Mr

of (address)

Signed (date)

*Authorised to sign

on behalf of (Adjoining Owner)

**Delete as appropriate*

ACKNOWLEDGEMENT OF PARTY STRUCTURE NOTICE

PARTY WALL ETC. ACT, 1996 SECTION 3

*I/We
of

having received the notice served
by
of

in respect of

which adjoins *my/our premises known as

*and in relation to the works proposed
under Section 2 Sub-section (2), paragraphs

*hereby consent to the above works
or
*hereby dissent from the above works and *concur in the appointment of/appoint as a surveyor
of (address)

Signed (date)
*Authorised to sign
on behalf of (Adjoining Owner)

**Delete as appropriate*

LETTER OF APPOINTMENT AS BUILDING OWNER'S SURVEYOR

From F. D. Dund
1 Nonsuch Road
London W.1

1 August 2000

Re Party Wall etc Act 1996
1/3 Nonsuch Road London W.1

Dear Mr Shaw,

As freehold owner of No. 1 I write to instruct you to act as my party wall surveyor in respect of the proposed works which I wish to carry out to the party wall between No. 1 and 3 Nonsuch Road.

I hereby authorise you to prepare, sign and serve any necessary notices under the Act on the adjoining owners/occupiers of No. 3 or other properties as appropriate.

I confirm your fee arrangement as set out in your letter of 15th July and appreciate I will be responsible for the costs involved arising from the service of the Notices.

Yours sincerely
F. Dund

Mr William A. A. Shaw, BSc, FRICS
Fresson & Tee
Chartered Surveyors
1 Sandwich Street
London WC1H 9PL

LETTER OF APPOINTMENT AS ADJOINING OWNER'S SURVEYOR

From A. A. Bell
15 Church Tower Street
London E.3

Re 15 Church Tower Street, London, E.3
Party Wall etc Act 1996

Dear Mr Shaw,

I enclose a copy of the Party Wall notice served on me by my neighbour in No. 17, Mr R. Edwards. Please act as my surveyor under the Party Wall etc Act and deal with the matter.

Following our telephone conversation I understand you wish to inspect the house and see for yourself if the works are covered by the Act and to establish that Mr. Edwards has the right to carry out the proposed works.

I confirm that if Mr Edwards does not meet your reasonable costs I will pay your reasonable fees.

Yours sincerely
Anthony A. Bell

Mr W. A. A. Shaw, BSc, FRICS
Fresson & Tee
Chartered Surveyors
1 Sandwich Street
London WC1H 9PL

PARTY WALL AWARD
AS MADE BETWEEN

AND

IN RESPECT OF

AND

FRESSON & TEE
CHARTERED SURVEYORS
1 SANDWICH STREET
LONDON WC1H 9PL

AN AWARD under the provisions of the Party Wall etc. Act 1996 to be served forthwith on the appointing owners, under Section 10(14)

WHEREAS

(Hereinafter referred to as the Building Owner) an owner within the meaning of the said Act of the premises known as

did on the day in the year 2000 serve upon

(hereinafter referred to as the Adjoining Owner) an owner within the meaning of the Act of the adjoining premises known as

notice of their intention to exercise the rights given to them under the Party Wall etc. Act 1996 Sections 1, 2(2) by executing works as more particularly defined in the Notice.

AND WHEREAS the Building Owner has appointed

to act as his surveyor and the Adjoining Owner has appointed

of to act as his Surveyor.

AND WHEREAS the two Surveyors so appointed have selected " " to act as Third Surveyor in accordance with the provisions of the Act or in the event of his being unable or unwilling to act and their being unable jointly to agree upon a substitute, they have agreed that another Third Surveyor shall be appointed by the Appointing Officer of the Local Authority NOW WE, being two of the three Surveyors so appointed, having inspected the said premises, DO HEREBY AWARD AND DETERMINE as follows:

1. (a) That the wall separating the Building and Adjoining Owner's premises is deemed to be a party wall/party fence wall within the meaning of the Act.
   (b) That the said wall as described in the attached schedule of condition is sufficient for the present purposes and needs of the Adjoining Owner.
   (c) That the Schedule of Condition dated attached hereto and signed by us the said two surveyors forms part of this Award.
   (d) That the drawings numbered. Attached hereto and signed by us the said two surveyors form part of this Award.

2. That fourteen days after the delivery of the signed Award the Building Owner shall be at liberty if he so chooses, but shall be under no obligation to carry out the following works:

   List of Works

3. That no material deviation from the agreed works shall be made without prior consultation with and agreement by the Adjoining Owner's Surveyor.

4. That if the Building Owner exercises the above rights he shall:–

   (a) Execute the whole of the aforesaid works at the sole cost of the Building Owner.
   (b) Take all reasonable precautions and provide all necessary support to retain the Adjoining Owner's land and buildings.
   (c) Make good forthwith all structural or decorative damage to the Adjoining Owner's building occasioned by the said works in materials to match the existing works.
   (d) Hold the Adjoining Owner free from liability in respect of any injury or loss of life to any person or damage to property caused by, or in consequence of, the execution of the said works and the costs of making any justified claims.
   (e) Permit the Adjoining Owner's Surveyor to have access to the Building Owner's premises at all reasonable times during the progress of the said works.
   (f) Carry out the whole of the said works, so far as practicable from the Building Owner's side. Where access to the Adjoining Owners premises adjacent to the Party Wall required reasonable notice shall be given.
   (g) Remove any scaffolding or screens as soon as possible and clear away dust and debris from time to time as necessary.

5. That the Building Owner's Surveyor shall be permitted access to the Adjoining Owner's property from time to time during the progress of the works at reasonable times and after giving reasonable notice.

6. That the whole of the works referred to in this Award shall be executed in accordance with the Building Regulations and any other requirements of Statutory Authorities and shall be executed in a proper and workmanlike manner in sound and suitable materials in accordance with the terms of this Award to the reasonable satisfaction of the Adjoining Owner's Surveyor.

7. That the works shall be carried through with reasonable expedition after commencement and so as to avoid any unnecessary inconvenience to the Adjoining Owners or occupiers. In particular noisy works shall be restricted to between the hours of   excepting weekends and Bank Holidays when no works shall be executed.

8. That the signed Awards shall be delivered forthwith to the appointing owners by their respective Surveyors. An unsigned copy of the documents shall also be provided for the Adjoining Owner's Surveyor.

9. That the Building Owner shall pay the Adjoining Owner's Surveyors fee of £   + V.A.T. in connection with the preparation of this Award and subsequent inspections of the works. In the event of damage being caused or other contingencies or variations arising a further fee shall be payable calculated at a rate of £   per hour exclusive of V.A.T.

10. That the said Surveyors reserve the right to make and issue any further Award or Awards that may be necessary as provided in the said Act.
11. That this Award shall be null and void if the permitted works do not commence within 12 months from the date of this Award.
12. Nothing in this Award shall be held as conferring admitting or affecting any right to light or air or any other easement, which may affect the Adjoining Owner whatsoever.

IN WITNESS WHEREOF we have set our hands this day of One Thousand Nine Hundred and Ninety.

Surveyor to the Building Owner

WITNESS

Name:

Address:

Occupation:

Surveyor to the Adjoining Owner

WITNESS

Name:

Address:

Occupation:

SCHEDULE OF CONDITION

40 Barnaby Street London W1

Schedule of Condition of areas in No.40 on first, second and third floors abutting No.42 Barnaby Street London W1

FRESSON AND TEE
CHARTERED SURVEYORS
1 SANDWICH STREET
LONDON WC1H 9PL

3rd JULY 1999

40 BARNABY STREET LONDON W1

SCHEDULE OF CONDITION ABUTTING PARTY WALL

Schedule prepared on 3/7/1999. Weather dry and sunny

Third Floor		
Front Room		
Ceiling	Plasterboard painted.	Generally sound and good decorative order crack 500mm long at junction of ceiling and soffitt at 90° to party wall.
Walls	Solid plastered painted.	Generally sound and good decorative order.
Floor	Timber framed.	Floor slopes down to centre of house approximately 100mm framed floor construction likely.
Tenants fittings	Hi-fi gear and projection equipment on face of party wall	All sound.
Bathroom off Front Room		
Ceiling	Plasterboard painted.	Generally sound.

Walls	Solid plastered painted.	Generally sound.
Floor	Quarry tiles.	Generally sound.
Third Floor Rear		
Ceiling	Plasterboard painted.	Generally sound. Good decorative order.
Walls	Solid plasterboard painted.	Generally sound.
Joinery	Cupboards in front and rear corners.	Generally sound.
Floor	Timber framed.	150mm slope to centre of house.
Left Hand Cupboard		
Ceiling	Plasterboard painted.	Fair order.
Party wall	Plasterboard painted.	Fair order.
Cross wall	Timber framed plasterboard painted.	Generally sound. 2mm open hairline crack at high level, visible by party wall. Hairline crack in lower part of cupboard.
Second Floor		

Front Room		
Ceiling	Plasterboard painted.	Generally sound.
Walls	Solid plasterboard painted. Fireplace with open grate and carpeted.	Generally sound.
Floor	Timber framed carpeted.	Generally sound, but slopes down to centre of house.
Bathroom		
Ceiling	Plasterboard painted.	Generally sound.
Walls	Solid plasterboard painted, in part rear recess timber panelled and painted.	Generally sound. Disturbed where panel behind has been removed.
Floor	Ceramic tiles.	Generally sound.
Second Floor		
Rear Room		
Ceiling	Plasterboard painted.	Generally sound.
Walls	Timber panelled painted with old fireplace in rear corner panelled in.	Old, but decoratively sound.

Floor	Timber framed carpeted.	Generally sound, but floor slopes down to centre of No.40.
Rear Bathroom		
Ceiling	Plasterboard painted.	Generally sound.
Walls	Timber framed painted tiled over bath and behind WC.	Generally sound.
Floor	Timber framed and carpeted.	Generally sound.
First Floor Front Room		
Ceiling	Plasterboard painted with timber panelling/cornice at perimeter.	Generally sound. Plaster finish uneven adjoining rear end of the chimney breast.
Walls	Solid wall lined in timber panelled with large chimney breast. Two recesses at front and rear ends of chimney breast.	Old, but sound and in good decorative order. Chimney flue open. Uneven render and concrete finish on right hand side of chimney flue at 600mm above floor level.
Floor	Render painted hearth to chimney breast. Timber framed and carpet.	Fair but uneven finish to render. Generally sound.

Ceiling of rear recess	Boarded and painted.	Two old pipe holes in rear right hand corner.
Kitchen (rear first floor)		
Ceiling	Plasterboard with timber cornice.	Generally sound. Uneven/rippled edge along rear edge on old chimney breast. 300mm of lifting plaster between ceiling and cornice 500mm from left hand cross wall.
Walls	Timber panelled, tiled and covered in cupboards.	Sound where seen. Old panelling.
Floor	PVC welded sheeting on timber floor.	Generally sound.
Rear Laundry		
Ceiling	Plastered painted.	Damp stained in part from above. Generally sound
Walls	Solid plastered painted. Part tiled. Softboard panel on wall up to 1.3 metres from floor behind fridge.	Generally sound.
Floor	UPVC sheet floor on timber base floor.	Open joints to adjoining surfaces but generally sound.

Index

account
settlement 38
work carried out, of 37–8
adjacent excavation 17–21
3 metre rule 17
diagram 18
6 metre rule within 45 degrees 18
diagram 19
deemed 19
dispute, as to 20
notice of
consent 20
precedents 51–3
service 18, 19
validity 20, 21
owner
deemed 19
duties of building 19, 21, 22–3
entitlement of adjoining 19, 21
liability of building 21
adjoining occupier
meaning 41–2
adjoining owner
guidance for 48–9
meaning 41–2
work carried out solely by building owner, subsequent use by 36
appeal
County Court, to
award, against 32
appointing officer
meaning 42
Award
appeal against 32
costs incurred in obtaining 31
form of 30–1
issue of 30
meaning 30
precedent 65–8
service 31–2
boundary wall
diagram 6
on line of junction 3
disputes, dealing with 7
owner
duty to adjoining 5, 6, 7
rights of 6–7
procedure 5–6
building owner
guidance for 46–8
meaning 42
Building Regulations approval
works subject to 8

compensation 22–3
loss or damage, for 7, 22, 35
conservation area, effect of 5
construction
adjacent 17–21
3 metre rule 17
diagram 18
6 metre rule within 45 degrees 18
diagram 19
deemed 19
dispute, as to 20
notice of
content 20
precedents 51–3
service 18, 19
validity 20, 21
owner
deemed 19
duties of building 19, 21, 22–3
entitlement of adjoining 19, 21
liability of building 21
on line of junction 3–7
adjoining owner's consent 4, 5
disputes, dealing with 7
expenses, as to 4, 5, 7, 32–3
owner
duty to adjoining 4, 5

rights of 6–7
over the line of junction 4
wholly on owner's land 3, 5–7
Control of Pollution Act notices 22
control of working methods 22
costs
dispute, arising out of 31
counter notices 15–16
avoidance 15
compliance 15
content 15
service 15
work carried out under expenses of 35
County Court
jurisdiction 32
Crown
application to the 41

damage
making good
expenses of 7, 22, 35
deemed compliance 14
dispute
actual 26
award
appeal against 32
conclusive 32
determining 30–1
dealing with 7, 17
deemed 26
expenses, as to 33
reasonable costs arising out of 31
resolution 26–32
award, by 30–2
surveyors' role 26–32
see also surveyors
disrepair
effect of 9
expenses as to 33, 34

easements 25–6
entry
notice of proposed requirements for 24–5
rights of
building owner, of 24
premises closed, where 24
surveyor, of 25
workmen, of 24
exemptions 40–1
expenses
building owner 32–3
making good damage, of 35
party fence wall, of 33
party wall, of 33
responsibility for 32–6
security for 36–8
external wall of building, repair of 8–14

fines 40
flashing
cutting into adjoining wall 11, 13
foundation
meaning 42

history 1–2

Inns of Court
exemption for 40–1

light
rights of 25–6
line of junction
interpretation 3
notice 55–6
listed buildings
consent requirements 8
effect of 5, 13
London Building Acts (Amendment) Act, 1939
re-enactment 1

Magistrates' Court
jurisdiction 40

notices
entry, intention of 24–5

line of junction 55–6
party structure 14–15, 57–60
see also party structure notices
precedents 51–68
service of 39
3 metre/6 metre 51–2
acknowledgement 53

offences 39–40
overview 1–2
owner
meaning 43

party fence wall
diagram 4
expenses as to 33, 34
height, as to 11, 34
meaning 43
party wall, as 11
procedure to build 4
repair of 8–14
party structure
cutting into 10, 13
demolition 9, 12–13
expenses as to 34
exposure of 12
meaning 43
rebuilding 9, 12–13
party structure notices 14–15, 57–60
acknowledgement of 57
consent to 15
content 14
dangerous 15
precedents 57–60
service 14–15
party wall
award
precedent 65–8
connecting to adjoining premises 11
definitions 44
expenses as to 33, 34
exposure of 12
height, as to 11, 13, 34
meaning 44
repair of 8–14
precedents 51–74
projections
cutting away 10, 13

raising
duties where no disrepair 12
rights 8
recovery of sums 40
repair
on line of junction 8–14
rights of entry 24–5
building owner, of 24
premises closed, where 24
surveyor, of 25
workmen, of 24

schedule of condition
precedent 69–74
Secretary of State
powers of 46
short title/commencement/extent 46
special foundations
costs 35–6
meaning 23, 45
specific agreement required 23
surveyors
adjoining owner, of
guidance for 48–9
letter of appointment 63
agreed
appointment of 26
award issued by 30
incapacity to act
effect of 27–8
settlement by award 30
appointment of 26–7
letter 61, 63
neglect, effect of 28, 29
refusal, effect of 28, 29
rescission, no 27
writing, in 27, 61, 63

award by
issue of 30
service of 31–2
building owner, of
letter of appointment 61
death of
effect of 28
ex parte procedure 28–9
incapacity to act
effect of 27
meaning 45
replacement of 28
responsibility of 27
settlement by award 30
third
appointment of 26, 29
award
issue 30
service 31
incapacity to act, effect of 29–30

thickening
duties where no disrepair 12
rights 8
Town and Country Planning Acts
effect of 8, 22

underpinning
duties where no disrepair 12
extent of 8
rights 8

works executed
agreement between owners, as to 23
statutory provisions, as to 23